973.9
CRA

20TH CENTURY USA

History of the 1950s

Rennay Craats

WEIGL PUBLISHERS INC.

Published by Weigl Publishers Inc.
123 South Broad Street, Box 227
Mankato, MN, USA   56002
Web site: http://www.weigl.com

Library of Congress Cataloging-in-Publication Data available upon request
from the publisher. Fax (507) 388-2746 for the attention of the Publishing
Records Department.

ISBN 1-930954-24-7

Printed and bound in the United States of America
1 2 3 4 5 6 7 8 9 0   05 04 03 02 01

Senior Editor
Jared Keen

Series Editor
Carlotta Lemieux

Copy Editor
Heather Kissock

Layout and Design
Warren Clark
Carla Pelkey

Photo Research
Joe Nelson

Photograph Credits
Anne Frank Fonds, Basel/Anne Frank House, Amsterdam/Archive Photos:
pages 3B, 24; APA/Archive Photos: page 19T; Archive Photos: pages 6BL, 7BL,
7BR, 14, 16, 18, 21, 26, 28, 31, 32, 33, 40, 41T, 41B; Bettmann/CORBIS: pages
15T, 15M, 20, 29, 42, 43; Camera Press Ltd./Archive Photos: page 17ML, 34;
George Meany Memorial Archives: page 35; Charles "Teenie" Harris/Archive
Photos: page 23; Hebgen Lake Ranger District: page 8; Hulton-Deutsch
Collection/CORBIS: page 17TR; Hulton Ghetty/Archive Photos: pages 19B, 25;
Kansas State Historical Society: page 9; Lookout Mountain Laboratory, USAF:
page 27; Carlos Marentes/The Bracero Project: pages 3MR, 38; Photofest: pages
3TL, 6BR, 10, 11T, 11B, 12, 13T, 13B, 36; Photo File/Archive Photos: page 30;
Popperfoto/Archive Photos: pages 22, 37.

Every reasonable effort has been made to trace ownership and to obtain permission to reprint
copyright material. The publishers would be pleased to have any errors or omissions brought
to their attention so that they may be corrected in subsequent printings.

USA 1950s Contents

Soviets in Space

War in Korea

Warsaw Pact Signed

HULA HOOPS

Mount Everest Conquered

Mau Mau Conflict

McCarthy Hearings

Hawai'i Joins Union

Piltdown Hoax

Larsen Pitches Perfect Game

The fifties were years of progress and change. Medical discoveries helped save lives, with advances in transplants and in the prevention of diseases such as polio. New suburban neighborhoods popped up to house the families of the baby boom. Even television centered on families, with hit shows such as *Leave it to Beaver*. Children spent their time watching Disney programs, spinning hula hoops, and playing with the most popular doll in history—Barbie. Teenagers looked to Hollywood and rock and roll for idols. James Dean and Buddy Holly became heroes, especially after their deaths.

The country itself changed as it added two new states to the Union. Americans looked to their presidents to keep the country prosperous and stable. This was difficult, as racial tensions exploded, and the economy fell in the late 1950s after a boom period. Communism also played a factor in fifties life. Senator

Union Wields Power

Kansas Floods

Anne Frank's Diary Found

We Like Ike!

Shopping Mall Built

Elvis Causes Uproar

ALBRIGHT TRIUMPHS

Quiz Show Fraud

Street Gangs

McCarthy launched his investigations to uncover communists living in the U.S. His efforts destroyed lives and careers. There was also a warming and refreezing in the Cold War between the USSR and the U.S. Communism squared off against democracy in events such as the Korean War.

The 1950s were fascinating years with equally fascinating characters. *20th Century USA: History of the 1950s* provides a selection of the many important events that helped shape U.S. history. There are many other fifties stories that you can discover at your local library. Countless books and newspaper articles have been written about the events and people of this decade. The Internet is also a great resource to find more information. For the time being, read on and experience the "cool" and "crazy" fifties for yourself.

1950

Charles Schultz enjoys working for *Peanuts*. His comic strip is a huge success. Find out why on page 11.

1950

North and South Korea face off in the Korean War. How did the U.S. get involved? Find out on page 16.

1950

No one is safe from McCarthy's hearings. The nation is stunned by the senator's hunt for communists. Find out what happened on page 21.

1951

Edward R. Murrow can *See It Now*. This newsman and his gutsy program are a hit on television. Learn more about them on page 12.

1951

Iran nationalizes the Anglo-Iranian Oil Company. Read about the resulting boycott and **coup** on page 42.

1951

An amendment is added to the Constitution. This change alters politics. Find out to what extent on page 21.

1952

The U.S. loves Lucy. Discover how Lucille Ball became a lasting Hollywood legend on page 11.

1952

Londoners cannot see with all the fog. Learn more about this killer mist on page 17.

1952

Dwight Eisenhower runs for president, but it is not all smooth sailing. Read about the snag along the way on page 22.

1953

The highest peak in the world has Edmund Hillary and Tensing Norgay celebrating. Find out where they were and what was accomplished on page 19.

1953

Americans sing in the rain with Gene Kelly. The musical film delights and entertains audiences. To read more about adding sound to silent movies, turn to page 10.

1954

U.S. parents breathe easier, thanks to the work of Dr. Jonas Salk. Find out how he contributed to children's health around the world on page 26.

1954

Disneyland is a hit show and a fashion setter. Find out how Davy Crockett became part of children's wardrobes on page 26.

The Korean War

Singin' in the Rain

1954

It is a fantasy world, according to J.R.R. Tolkien. His books about wizards, hobbits, and dragons wow the world. Discover more about the first book in the trilogy on page 25.

1955

Movie fans are stunned by the death of a hero. James Dean dies in a car accident. Find out more about this rebel on page 12.

1955

New England is rocked by Hurricane Diane. This is not a usual storm. Learn about it on page 8.

1956

Mickey Mantle is on top. To read more about this star Yankee who led the league, turn to page 30.

1956

Autherine Lucy is allowed to go to school. See what makes this monumental on page 32.

1956

A boxing legend retires. What made Rocky Marciano such a star? Turn to page 31 to find out.

1957

Soviets set their sights on space. They take a step in the right direction in October. Page 19 has more about how a dog brings them closer to their goal of space exploration.

1957

The Cleavers invade U.S. living rooms, and Americans love it! They cannot get enough of the Beaver. Find out more on page 13.

1958

The answers are revealed, and U.S. television viewers are not impressed. Learn why a teacher came under fire about a game show on page 11.

1958

Americans are caught up with plastic hoops. Discover why they were swiveling their hips on page 14.

1958

Students are near the end of their day when their school catches on fire. Many students escape the burning building. Some do not. Learn more about this disaster on page 9.

1959

The newest American is a young girl's best friend. Barbie takes the country, and the world, by storm. Find out more on page 14.

1959

Yellowstone National Park shakes violently on August 17. The results are deaths and Earthquake Lake. Learn more on page 8.

1959

Three music legends lose their lives in a plane crash. See what happened on page 41.

Rocky Marciano

Buddy Holly

Landslide and Earthquake

A powerful earthquake rumbled through campsites in Montana's Yellowstone National Park just before midnight on August 17, 1959. The shock loosened rock, dirt, and trees, creating a landslide down the slope of the Madison River Canyon. A 2,000-foot-long and 1,300-foot-wide chunk of the ridge fell into the canyon. The debris blocked the river and created a dam. The dam caused the river to flood cottages, forests, and sections of the highway that ran through the canyon. The water eventually settled into a 175-foot-deep lake called Earthquake Lake. The slide sealed some geysers and springs, and created others. Some surviving geysers changed their pattern for many months after the disaster. Old Faithful, which had a regular schedule of eruptions, was erratic and unpredictable. Some springs' temperatures rose 6° Fahrenheit. Twenty-eight people were killed in the rock slide, most of whom were campers and vacationers.

■ The Yellowstone earthquake of 1959 caused major physical changes to the area.

Hurricane Diane

Hurricane Diane hit New England in August 1955. It was not the strongest storm the U.S. had endured in terms of wind speed and sea action. However, it became the country's first billion-dollar hurricane because of the incredible flooding caused by heavy rains. A previous storm, Hurricane Connie, had already filled the river systems and water table. Hurricane Diane brought heavy rains so quickly that warnings could not be issued fast enough. In Stroudsburg, Pennsylvania, Brodhead Creek rose 30 inches in only fifteen minutes. This rapid flooding drowned fifty people. Connecticut rivers swelled, growing to between three and five times their usual size. In Winsted, 12 feet of water swept through the town. Huge sections of towns were completely destroyed, and a chemical plant in Putnam spilled magnesium into the river. Flaming water then flowed through the city. In Woonsocket, Rhode Island, coffins from local graveyards floated through town after being unearthed by the storm's power. Throughout the region, severe flooding and damage occurred.

Hurricane Diane trapped thousands of tourists in resorts across New England. More than 190 people were killed, and damage was estimated at $1.6 to $1.8 billion. It was the most expensive natural disaster in U.S. history.

Twister Tragedy

On June 9, 1953, newspaper reporter John Sorgini and photographer Howard Smith saw a dark funnel in the sky near Worcester, Massachusetts. Within a minute, a tornado touched down in the city's north end. The power of the twister tore a 40-mile-long path through the center of the state, throwing debris to Boston 40 miles to the east. A residential area, a college campus, and a new housing project were completely flattened. Many of the victims at the housing project were children. A new $6 million factory that had opened only days before was destroyed. Another smaller funnel cloud tore through some of the surrounding smaller towns. About 94 people died immediately, and an estimated 1,306 were wounded. The twister caused more than $53 million in damage, making it the most expensive tornado to date and the worst in New England history.

Flooding in Kansas

The weather in July 1951 was beginning to worry people. Kansas had received unusually high amounts of rain for two months. Four straight days of storms then produced more water than the area could handle. The region flooded. On July 13, the flood crested at Topeka and Lawrence, Kansas, and at Kansas City, Missouri. More than 850,000 acres of corn and wheat were under water. About one-quarter of Topeka's residents were evacuated for their safety. A great deal of Kansas City was already covered in floodwater. Oil storage tanks then exploded and, despite so much water, fires burned for nearly a week. About 200,000 people were forced to leave their homes. The flood caused more than $1 billion in

■ Floodwaters covered much of Kansas City and outlying areas.

damage. Forty-one people drowned in the flooding, but the death toll could have been much higher.

SCHOOL NIGHTMARE

■ Students had only thirty-five minutes of classes left on December 1, 1958, when a fire was discovered at Our Lady of Angels School in Chicago, Illinois. More than 1,200 students were attending classes. Two teachers smelled smoke and led their classes out of the school even before the fire alarm sounded. Students on the first floor were helped out of the building by passersby and school personnel. A math teacher on the second floor barricaded his door with books and waited for firefighters to arrive with ladders to rescue him and his students. Those studying on the third floor were not as lucky. Ninety-two students and three nuns were trapped in the fire and died. It was discovered later that the fire had been set deliberately. The **arsonist** was never found. In 1979, however, a person called a Chicago radio talk show and confessed to setting this and several other fires in the city.

Singin' in the Rain

A 1953 smash hit, *Singin' in the Rain*, had fans singing in sunshine as well as rain. The musical story of a film studio's switch from silent to talking pictures was full of laughs, love, and great songs. Most of the laughs were courtesy of Donald O'Connor's physical comedy. He won the Golden Globe for Best Actor in a Musical or Comedy for his performance. The story followed silent-film stars Don Lockwood, played by Gene Kelly, and Lina Lamont, played by Jean Hagan, as they tried to master the new entertainment—talking pictures. But talking posed a serious problem for the successful duo. Lamont had a terrible, squeaky voice. Chorus girl Kathy Seldon, played by Debbie Reynolds, stepped in to record her beautiful speaking and singing voice over the star's. In the process, Lockwood and Seldon fell in love. One of the most memorable scenes in the film also provided its title—after realizing he was in love with Seldon, Lockwood splashed and danced while singing in the rain.

■ *Singin' in the Rain* remains popular after nearly fifty years.

Dragnet

The crime cases tackled by the Los Angeles Police Department inspired one of the greatest shows in the 1950s. *Dragnet* was the first "reality" television program. The drama featured police officers Joe Friday, played by Jack Webb, and Frank Smith, played first by Herb Ellis and then by Ben Alexander, as they tried to solve crimes. *Dragnet* presented the truth behind crime fighting. Throughout the show, Friday and Smith asked for "just the facts," a phrase that lived on long after the show ended.

Webb was more than the star of the show. He wrote many of the scripts and directed the program as well. In the 1953-54 season, *Dragnet* was second only to *I Love Lucy* in ratings.

TELEVISION GOES COLOR

■ For the few Americans with color television sets, NBC offered regular programming in color in 1953. Many viewers were not sold on the idea of color television. The sets cost a lot—between $500 and $1,000—and the pictures were often warped. The colors bled on television, and viewers had to adjust the knobs constantly in order to get the right color.

Programming in full color was only available for two hours each day, mostly on NBC. Its **affiliate**, RCA, made all-color picture tubes. Black and white television remained popular until the 1960s, when color sets began to take over the market.

Loving Lucy

It did not take long for a spoof on married life to hit the top in 1951. By the end of *I Love Lucy's* first six months in 1952, the comedy show was number one in the ratings. Within a year, the cast, including Lucille Ball and her husband Desi Arnez, negotiated the biggest television contract to date— they signed for $8 million. The network knew the show was a good investment. *I Love Lucy* drew 50 million viewers every Monday night.

The plot of the show often mirrored Ball's personal life. The writers timed her television pregnancy with her real-life one in 1954. This hit the front pages of U.S. newspapers. So did the famous couple's divorce in 1960, which put the show on hold. But Ball had too much to offer show business to stop. Two years later, *The Lucille Ball Show* debuted.

■ Despite her bumbling antics, everyone loved Lucy.

It was later called *Here's Lucy*. It, too, rocketed to the top of the ratings. It stayed there until Ball decided to end the series in 1974.

Quiz Show

In the 1950s, university teacher Charles Van Doren was seen as one of the smartest men on television. Millions of Americans tuned into the game show *Twenty-One* to watch him match wits with another contestant. Van Doren faced questions about everything from baseball to opera. He eliminated opponent after opponent and walked away from *Twenty-One* a hero, winning a record $129,000.

In 1958, Van Doren's hero status was taken away. That year, a previous contestant told the New York District Attorney's office that the show was fixed. The city launched an investigation of other game shows and found **fraud** in many of them. At the inquiry, Van Doren at first denied being part of the deception. Then he admitted it and tried to convince people how sorry he was. He was disgraced, lost his job, and moved to Chicago.

NUTS FOR PEANUTS

■ In October 1950, Charlie Brown and his friends appeared in newspaper funny pages for the first time. The *Peanuts* gang was made up of strong-willed Lucy, her blanket-toting brother Linus, piano-playing Schroeder, the self-conscious Charlie Brown, and his lovable dog, Snoopy. A parade of other characters, including Pigpen, Woodstock, and Peppermint Patty, made appearances in the strip's

© 1950, 1965, 1983 United Feature Syndicate, Inc.

■ Charlie Brown, Snoopy, and Woodstock have been appearing in newspapers for more than five decades.

frames. The characters were often faced with real-life situations, such as disappointment and triumph.

Six newspaper syndicates turned Charles Schultz down before one finally gave him a chance. Since then, *Peanuts* has appeared in more than 2,000 papers in more than 20 languages. Schultz won several awards for his cartoons, including the National Cartoonist Society's Reuben award in 1955 and 1964. Schultz continued drawing *Peanuts* until January 2000, and he died about a month later.

Death of a Hero

Twenty-four-year-old James Dean was already a Hollywood legend by September 1955. His first movie, *East of Eden*, had been released that year, and his second, *Rebel Without a Cause*, was scheduled to hit theaters in October.

Dean had just finished filming another movie, *Giant*. On September 30, Dean was driving his Porche to Salinas, California, for a car race. A police officer stopped him and warned that if he did not slow down, he would never make it. The officer was right. Dean hit another car at a crossroads. The other driver had minor injuries, and Dean's passenger was thrown from the vehicle. The Hollywood star was not as lucky. The crash broke his neck, and he died instantly. Fans were shocked and devastated. The success of *Rebel Without a Cause* catapulted Dean into idol status. The dead star received 8,000 letters each week through the movie studio. Dean's style has been mimicked by many celebrities, but it has never been duplicated.

"To me, the only success, the only greatness, is immortality."

James Dean

Although James Dean died at a young age, his contributions to Hollywood live on.

Legendary Newsman

Edward R. Murrow was a respected radio celebrity before moving to television. Murrow's *Hear It Now* was adapted for television as *See It Now* in 1951. While many television personalities were reading press releases in front of the camera, Murrow brought stories alive. The show's documentaries were praised for their realistic and gutsy approach to controversial issues. Murrow explored the harsh tactics of Senator Joseph McCarthy's investigations. He also told viewers the story of an air force lieutenant whose career was destroyed by McCarthy's commission. The lieutenant was ruined not by his own beliefs or loyalties but by those of his sister and father. Five weeks after the program aired, the lieutenant was restored to duty. That year, *See It Now* won twenty awards.

THE TONIGHT SHOW

NBC's late-night talk show, *The Tonight Show*, premiered on September 27, 1954. Steve Allen was the show's original host. His dry and casual approach made him a fan favorite. The show was a huge success. Every night, *The Tonight Show* invited singers and comedians to entertain American audiences. Jack Paar, a popular interviewer, took over the show in 1957. His sense of humor gave the program an edge. One of the show's best-known hosts, Johnny Carson, came on board in 1962. For thirty years, Carson appeared after the announcer cued, "Here's Johnny!" He became an important part of popular culture and, on retiring, handed the reins to comedian Jay Leno. *The Tonight Show* remained popular into the twenty-first century.

Disney Mania

Nineteen fifty-five was a great year for Walt Disney. His television series, *Disneyland*, was at the top of the ratings. The program's "Frontierland" segment was an incredible success. Then Disneyland, "the happiest place on Earth," opened its doors in Anaheim, California, in July. The amusement park cost $17 million to build and covered 160 acres. It was the first park of its kind. The "Magic Kingdom" had attractions and rides to suit every member of the family. Given the incredible crowds

■ Mousketeers pledged allegience to the flag and a cartoon mouse.

during the opening week, there were immediate thoughts of expansion. Other Disney theme parks were later built in Florida, Japan, and France.

Walt Disney achieved another amazing feat in 1955. That October, he introduced a children's television show. The after-school program was called *The Mickey Mouse Club*, and the children on the show were Mouseketeers. They became huge celebrities and icons of the fifties, and the show carried on through the rest of the century.

Family Values

Fifties television was packed with shows about families. *Leave It to Beaver* debuted in 1957. It followed the lives of the middle-class Cleavers—June, Ward, and their children Wally and Theodore, better known as Beaver. Every week, the children found themselves in messes they could not get out of. Their parents helped them make things right and taught them lessons on the way. After 234 episodes, *Leave It to Beaver* went off the air. Loyal watchers gathered around their televisions to say goodbye to their favorite TV family on September 12, 1963.

When *Father Knows Best* was first aired on October 3, 1954, it was not successful. CBS cancelled it. A flood of angry

■ Comedies such as *Father Knows Best* served as models of the ideal U.S. family.

letters convinced NBC to pick up the show and move it to an earlier time so families could watch together. It became a hit. The *Father Knows Best* family was one that Americans wanted to imitate. In the 1959-60 season,

Father Knows Best had its best year. It ranked sixth among all shows on television. By the end of the year, Robert Young, who played the father, Jim, wanted to leave the program. The show came to an end at its most popular time. It was shown in reruns for another two seasons, and the last show was aired on April 5, 1963.

Beatniks

◼ A group of beatniks gather to share poetry and music.

The "Beat Generation" came out of the 1950s. Many of these people had fought in the Korean War and did not believe in the American Dream anymore. "Beat," to them, meant beaten. The beatniks originated in San Francisco and Los Angeles. They were easy to spot. The men wore beards and short hair. They usually sported khaki pants, sweaters, and sandals. Women wore black leotards or long dresses. Beatniks loved jazz and wrote poetry, and they often read it in coffee houses with drums or other instruments accompanying them.

Jack Kerouac was a leader who tried to explain that the beatniks loved everything and were not the radicals the "squares" thought they were. He wrote one of the most famous beat books, *On the Road*, which sold 500,000 copies. The book is about friendship and wanderings, and Kerouac wrote it in just three weeks.

Hula Hoop

In 1958, a California toymaker caught wind of an Australian game used in gym classes—students exercised by spinning bamboo hoops around their waists. The toymaker decided to try it in the U.S. From the moment they began selling, the $1.98 hula hoops were a phenomenon. Within six months, 30 million hoops were sold. The fad started in California and quickly worked its way across the country. A 10-year-old boy in New Jersey set a record with 3,000 consecutive spins. The country was hoop-crazy, and it was not only children getting in on the fun. Adults spun the hoops, too. People could not get enough of hula hoops, for a while, at least. Like any fad, this one soon lost its popularity. The end of the summer brought the end of the craze. Children still played with hula hoops, but they were no longer a must-have.

BARBIE

◼ In March 1959, children had a new playmate. Mattel Toys launched their new toy doll named Barbie. The 11.5-inch doll sold for $3.00. As sales of the doll rocketed, different Barbies were released, all with different clothing and accessories. Barbie was given a boyfriend, Ken, in 1961 and then many friends in the years to come. Barbie has become the most successful doll in history, selling hundreds of millions of dolls around the world.

Slang

bread money

hip cool, knows what is going on

wheels a car

cat a male

airhead empty-headed

flip to become enthusiastic

crazy the most, wonderful

drop dead go away, get lost

3-D Movies

In 1952, the movie industry found that its audiences had been reduced by about half because people were watching the new invention, television. Movie producers needed a way to draw people back to the theaters. It found one. The National Vision Corporation thought up a movie idea called **three-dimensional**, or 3-D. By projecting overlapping images onto the screen, the company made the pictures look as if the action were happening right there. This only worked if the audience wore Polaroid glasses that brought the images back together again.

The first full-length 3-D movie was shown in Los Angeles on November 26, 1952. *Bwana Devil* made a record $95,000 in its first week. Audiences loved the effect of characters jumping out at them. The fad exploded in the U.S. and then faded quickly. The novelty of 3-D movies could no longer support the low-budget plots, so studios stopped producing them.

■ Special 3-D glasses allowed moviegoers to become part of the action.

College Cramming

■ The popularity of cramming reached its peak in the late fifties.

In the 1950s, college cramming had nothing to do with studying. Students would try to stuff as many bodies as possible into the tightest places. Across the country, college campuses were packed with students trying to set records by fitting as many people or objects as possible in the smallest space possible. At one California college, twenty-two students managed to stuff themselves into a phone booth. At another, forty students filled a Volkswagon Beetle. At Caltech, two students filled their room with newspaper. This crazy spring tradition swept the U.S. in the late fifties and was abandoned in the sixties.

DANCE FLOOR DYNAMOS

■ The fifties were a great time for dancing. There were many different dances that often went with the hit songs of the time. The hand jive, danced to a song of the same name, was a series of claps, hand movements, foot steps, and kicks. Like most dances of the decade, the hand jive was often done with a partner. Jiving came out of the energetic jitterbug dancing of the 1940s. The jive was a slightly tamer version of the forties dance but just as much fun for dancers. Many complicated moves, turns, and flips were put together and performed to rock-and-roll music.

Other dances were novelties. The stroll was a dance performed with the help of foot-shaped cutouts placed on the floor for the dancers to follow. The slop, the bop, and the mashed potato were other fun dance crazes in the fifties.

■ Millions of people died in the three-year war between North and South Korea.

Korean War

For five years, Korea had been split into Soviet-backed North Korea and U.S.-backed South Korea. On June 25, 1950, the North invaded the South. U.S. General Douglas MacArthur led the United Nations (UN) forces that went to South Korea to defend it. By October, the UN had pushed the communist troops of the North back nearly to the Chinese border. Communist China then became involved, and the fighting **escalated**. Peace negotiations failed in 1951 because the sides disagreed on where the line dividing the two Koreas should be. The sides also disagreed on whether all prisoners captured by the South should be sent back to the North. Many of the 132,000 prisoners were non-communists who had been forced to fight for the North. The UN would only return those who wanted to go. The North refused the terms, and the war raged on.

In June 1953, an agreement was close when South Korean President Syngman Rhee ordered his troops to disregard any treaties reached during the negotiations. He also organized the "escape" of 25,000 prisoners who did not want to return to the North. The communist North reacted with brutal attacks. The U.S. pressured Rhee to cooperate, and the treaty was finally signed on July 27. Casualties on both sides had been high. Little land had changed hands, and about 4 million people had died— nearly 2 million Koreans, 1 million Chinese, 54,000 Americans, and several thousand other UN troops.

WARSAW PACT

■ Post-war Europe was taking shape in the 1950s. The Paris Agreements of 1954 allowed West Germany to become a member of the North Atlantic Treaty Organization (NATO). It joined the U.S., Canada, Great Britain, and most other countries of Western Europe in this military alliance. The USSR feared that West Germany would now rebuild its military. The USSR had been the victim of German aggression twice in forty years. The USSR and its communist allies met in Warsaw to discuss what to do to protect themselves. They agreed on a "mutual assistance treaty" on May 14, 1955. Albania, Bulgaria, Czechoslovakia, East Germany, Hungary, Poland, Romania, and the USSR promised to come to each other's aid immediately if attacked. The Warsaw Pact gave the USSR an excuse to move military units into its allies' countries.

Apartheid in South Africa

Apartheid in South Africa existed before Prime Minister Daniel Francois Malan and the Nationalist Party took control in 1948. But in 1950, the government installed specific policies and made apartheid legal. Every person in the country was classified as belonging to one of four racial groups: black, white,

■ South Africa's apartheid policies greatly limited the rights of non-white citizens.

colored or mixed race, and Asian. The Group Areas Act separated cities into racial districts. Apartheid laws set out which jobs members of each race could hold and what level of education they could receive. Non-whites were not allowed in government, and marriage between different races was prohibited. The government introduced strict legislation surrounding apartheid. As a result, life became very difficult for non-whites. Thousands of people died fighting apartheid. Apartheid officially ended in 1990, but the results of the policy are still widespread.

Fogged In

In the winter of 1952, London, England, was buried beneath a blanket of fog. This was no ordinary fog—it was caused by pollution. London's factories and the coal fires in peoples' homes released about 2,000 tons of sulfur dioxide and other **toxic** substances into the air every day. In December, an uncommon weather system trapped the pollutants close to the ground.

■ Thick clouds of smog blanketed the streets of London, prompting tougher pollution laws.

For three weeks, the sky went from yellow to black. People could see only a few feet in front of them. They called the toxic fog "smog." The smog killed 4,000 people, and another 8,000 later died of respiratory problems. This environmental disaster opened people's eyes to the dangers of pollution.

Stalin Dead

The man who had ruled the USSR with an iron fist died on March 5, 1953, at the age of 73. People did not know if they should celebrate or mourn Joseph Stalin's passing. During twenty-nine years of leadership, Stalin had won wars and industrialized the country. He had also ordered mass murders and forced **collectivization**. Russians waited to see what would happen next. Several of Stalin's top advisors carefully competed for leadership. Lavrenti Beria began plotting to take over, but the head of the Communist Party's central committee, Nikita Khrushchev, had other ideas. Khrushchev soon emerged as one of the most powerful men in the government. Khrushchev and Georgi Malenkov, chairman of the Council of Ministers, joined to stop Beria from taking control of the country. They arrested Beria in July for being a part of Stalin's terrorism and executed him shortly after. Not only did this get rid of an opponent, but it also sent a message to Soviets that Stalinism would not be tolerated. Khrushchev took small steps towards de-Stalinizing the USSR and giving its people more freedom. He became premier in 1958.

■ Joseph Stalin is carried to his final resting place.

French Lose War in Vietnam

The end of the war between France and Vietnam was marked by the Battle of Dienbienphu. French General Henri Navarre wanted to lure the **Viet Minh** into fighting conventional instead of **guerrilla** warfare. In November 1953, French soldiers took over the village of Dienbienphu and set up a fortress. General Navarre hoped that the Viet Minh would storm toward them across the valley and be easy targets. With the mountains surrounding them, Navarre felt it would be impossible to bring big weapons to this area.

He was wrong. About 200,000 Vietnamese took apart weapons and carried the pieces on their backs to Dienbienphu. The Viet Minh then tunneled under the fortress walls to attack. By March 1954, the village was a war zone. The U.S. offered air raids but did not get involved on the ground. On May 7, the Viet Minh took back Dienbienphu. French Premier Joseph Laniel was replaced by Pierre Mendès-France. The new leader promised to negotiate a **cease-fire**. The war was over by July, and Vietnam was independent. After eight years of fighting, 1.3 million Vietnamese and 95,000 French soldiers were dead.

PAPA DOC

■ Since the former leader of Haiti, Paul Magloire, was forced to resign in 1956, the country had been in turmoil. Six **provisional** presidents in ten months had failed to bring order to the unstable country. Physician François Duvalier, known as "Papa Doc," led the opposition against Magloire. In September 1957, he was elected to a six-year presidential term. He promised to control the army and get rid of the ruling class. After a coup attempt in 1958, Papa Doc created a secret police force called the Tontons Macoutes, which is **Creole** for "boogeymen." These personal soldiers murdered and tortured people. Anyone who opposed Duvalier was killed.

MOUNT EVEREST CONQUERED

■ At 11:30 AM on May 29, 1953, New Zealander Edmund Hillary and his guide Tensing Norgay looked out from the top of Mount Everest on the Nepal-Tibet border. They were the first people to climb to the mountain's peak. Hillary had tried once before to make it to the summit, and Norgay had attempted the climb seven times before, but neither had made it.

When they finally reached the peak, the men stayed only fifteen minutes. They planted British, Nepalese, and UN flags, took some photographs, and then headed back down. Mount Everest stands 29,028 feet above sea level and is the highest point on the planet.

Soviets in Space

On October 4, 1957, the Soviets launched a satellite called *Sputnik I* into orbit around Earth. This satellite weighed 185 pounds and traveled at about 17,400 miles per hour. Each revolution took 96.17 minutes. The first satellite sent into space excited people around the world. Later that year, a dog named Laika became the first living creature to orbit Earth. Laika was launched by the Soviets on November 3 aboard *Sputnik II*. Scientists set up food and drink and an oxygen tank so that she could breathe. From Earth, they measured her pulse, breathing, and movement to see how animals react in space. They used what they learned from Laika to plan a human space mission.

■ Laika, the first dog in space, provided important data to scientists.

Mau Mau Conflict

Most Kenyans wanted independence from Britain. The Kikuyu, members of the country's largest ethnic group, took to physical action in 1951. By the following year, a secret society called the Mau Mau launched a violent campaign against both the British and the Africans who supported the British. In October 1952, the colonial governor announced a state of emergency and sent troops to Kenya to stop the rebellion. Jomo Kenyatta, the leader of the largely Kikuyu party called the Kenya African National Union, was arrested. He was charged with being responsible for the Mau Mau attacks. In 1953, he was sentenced to seven years in jail.

■ Soldiers escort Jomo Kenyatta to a Kenyan courthouse for trial.

Fighting continued for another three years. By the end of the revolt, 11,000 Mau Mau rebels were dead and 80,000 Kikuyu men, women, and children had been held in detention camps. About 2,000 pro-British Africans and 100 Europeans were killed.

The Mau Mau rebellion brought African issues into the open, and efforts to address some of the grievances led to Kenya's independence in 1963. The following year, Kenyatta became the country's first president.

Political Television

The 1952 Republican convention was the first ever to be aired on television. Three of the major networks sent thousands of journalists to cover the convention at Chicago's International Amphitheater. Americans enjoyed front-row seats in their own living rooms during the three weeks of vigorous campaigning. At-home spectators watched Eisenhower fight for the nomination and saw the disappointment of the losers first-hand. Television brought politics down to a level that Americans could

■ Millions of Americans were able to watch the 1952 Republican convention from the comfort of their homes.

access and understand. It captured political antics and strategies, including signs, buttons, and umbrellas, all printed with the Republican slogan—"I Like Ike," in reference to Eisenhower's nickname. Through television, millions of voters decided they liked Ike, too.

Crime Commission TV Craze

The best show on television was a true-life crime drama. In May 1950, Senator Estes Kefauver and his Special Committee to Investigate Organized Crime launched their probe. The committee traveled to six major cities questioning mafia bosses, criminals, and anyone else who could provide useful information. A key person in the investigation was Virginia Hill Hauser, mobster "Bugsy" Siegel's ex-girlfriend. She told the committee all about her extravagant lifestyle that was funded by the mafia. She would not say anything about the "business." Hauser's

information, along with her style, made her memorable. On her way out of the courtroom, she punched a reporter and yelled at the rest of them. The committee also put government officials in the hot seat. New York mayor William O'Dwyer defended himself against charges of corruption. He was accused of appointing mafia friends to important posts.

Kefauver and his committee did more than expose the seedy **underworld**. He and other committee members became stars. Movie theaters realized that people were staying home to watch the hearings rather than coming out to their shows. Theaters soon played the hearings instead of Hollywood movies on the big screen. After gathering evidence of ties between political leaders and crime organizations, Kefauver resigned from the committee in May 1951. He entered the Democratic presidential nominations the following year and was an unsuccessful vice-presidential candidate in 1956. He was re-elected to the Senate in 1954 and again in 1960.

> "The opening session of the Senate Crime Investigating Committee was nothing less than a Hollywood thriller truly brought to life. The central characters could hardly have been cast to type more perfectly."
>
> Jack Gould, *New York Times*

McCarthy Anti-communism

Despite the Allied victory in World War II, China, Hungary, and Czechoslovakia, remained communist. Some people thought U.S. officials had helped the communists. State Department employee Alger Hiss admitted to giving confidential information to the Soviets. In February 1950, Senator Joseph McCarthy, a Republican from Wisconsin, launched the House Un-American Activities Committee hearings. With fear of communism fueling his crusade, McCarthy announced that he had the names of 205 known communists working in the State Department. His charge was never backed up.

Regardless of the lack of evidence, McCarthy continued to accuse prominent Americans of being communists. People in all levels of U.S. society, from small business owners to Hollywood stars, faced being blacklisted and losing their jobs because of accusations in McCarthy's hearings. For four-and-a-half years, McCarthy bullied people and ruined lives. In 1954, he went too far. He turned his attack on the U.S. Army, and the resulting Army-McCarthy hearings were aired on television. People were shocked at how McCarthy treated witnesses called before him. Counsel for the Army, Joseph Welch, was soft-spoken and gentle. His behavior was an obvious contrast to McCarthy's loud accusations. Welch won Americans' support and ended McCarthy's run. Moderate Republicans joined with Democrats to **censure** McCarthy. The senator's power and career were over. He died in 1957.

■ Anti-communist feelings ran wild during the McCarthy era.

LIMITS OF POWER

■ Before 1951, a president could be elected every four years for as long as voters wished. There was no limit to how long a person could serve as the president of the U.S. President Roosevelt had served four terms in the White House before his death while in office in 1945. On February 27, 1951, the twenty-second amendment to the Constitution became law. This stated that a politician could not serve more than two terms as president. The new law did not apply to President Truman. The amendment stated that the president in office at the time of the amendment was not subject to the two-term rule. Still, Truman retired after serving two terms.

Business as Usual

In 1953, President Eisenhower appointed Charles E. Wilson Secretary of Defense. Wilson was president of General Motors and had long been involved in defense, but he was better at business than politics because he insisted on speaking his mind. He once said, "What is good for our country is good for General Motors, and vice versa." The comment was printed in every newspaper. It gave the feeling that Wilson was not as impartial as a government official should be. Despite this and other mistakes, he did a good job in the defense department. In 1957, when Wilson retired, the government lost not only a strong administrator but also one with style and personality.

The U.S. Likes Ike

Dwight Eisenhower decided to run for the Republican presidential nomination in 1952. It was a bitter fight between him and Robert Taft, but Eisenhower came out on top. He and running mate Richard Nixon were ready to face the challenges ahead. President Truman decided not to seek re-election, so the Democrats pitted Adlai Stevenson against Eisenhower. Eisenhower made Americans love him. He promised to "go to Korea" but did not say what he would do there. Americans who supported the war believed he would be aggressive, and those who wanted an end to the war believed he would pull out.

While Eisenhower was winning votes, Nixon was in hot water. Nixon was accused of accepting improper campaign contributions. He spoke on television about false charges, saying the only gift he had ever accepted from constituents was his dog, Checkers. Voters rallied behind Nixon, and the Republican team was stronger than ever. Eisenhower's down-to-earth personality helped Americans trust him. Television ads announced what many Americans were feeling—"I Like Ike." This simple slogan blew Stevenson's **lofty** speeches out of the water. In the election, the Republicans received 33 million votes—a record in peacetime.

■ Before becoming president, Eisenhower commanded the Allied armies during World War II.

MacArthur Brought Home

April 1951, President Truman called General Douglas MacArthur home from Korea and removed him from his military post. The two men had a history of not seeing eye-to-eye, and MacArthur had publicly criticized the president and his handling of the Korean War. MacArthur wanted Truman to declare war on China, which was attacking United Nations troops in Korea. The president wanted to prevent the situation from blowing up and becoming another world war. To ensure that the situation would be controlled, Truman ordered General MacArthur home and replaced him with Lieutenant General Matthew Ridgway.

"I have therefore considered it essential to relieve General MacArthur so that there would be no doubt or confusion as to the real purpose and aim of our policy."
President Harry Truman

Alaska and Hawai'i Join the Union

At the end of the fifties, the U.S. grew. It welcomed two new states—Alaska and Hawai'i—to the Union. Alaskans had been pushing for statehood for many years. In 1947, Congress had discussed Alaska's statehood and then passed the request in 1950. The Korean War caused the statehood measure to be shelved until after the war. In 1955, the territory's government drafted a state constitution, and Alaskans voted to accept it in 1956. On May 26, 1958, the U.S. government finally passed the Alaska statehood bill, and on July 7, 1958, President Eisenhower signed the measure into law. On January 3, 1959, Alaska officially became the forty-ninth U.S. state.

Hawai'i had tried to become a state since the early 1900s, but the U.S. government did not seriously consider the issue until the 1930s. Debates continued through that decade, but World War II halted the discussions. Hawai'i's efforts were linked to those of Alaska's. Advocates of Alaskan and Hawai'ian statehood helped push the measures through. In March 1959, the Hawai'ian bill was passed and signed by the president. On June 27, Hawai'ians voted to join the Union as the fiftieth and final state.

EISENHOWER RE-ELECTED

■ Eisenhower was a very popular president among citizens. His popularity in Congress, however, was not as strong. In 1954, the Republican Party lost control of Congress. Two years later, despite having had a heart attack, Eisenhower decided to run for a second term. He won in forty-one states, but the Democrats continued to control Congress. In 1957, Eisenhower proudly presented Congress and Americans with the third balanced budget in a row. Another recession hit the country, and Eisenhower's government did not move quickly enough to stop it from spreading and becoming worse. There was also evidence of financial corruption in the government. These factors led to a huge Democratic victory in the congressional elections of 1958.

A STRONG UNITED STATES NEEDS

STEVENSON

VOTE DEMOCRATIC [X]

Pittsburgh Outdoor Adv ©

■ Despite his intelligence, Stevenson was unable to compete with Eisenhower's popularity.

Intellectual Adlai

Adlai Stevenson was elected Governor of Illinois in 1947. He fought for reforms in such areas as education, health, and the civil service. In 1952, he was chosen as the Democratic nominee for the presidency. He soon found that he could not compete with Dwight Eisenhower's easygoing approach. Stevenson was an Ivy-league intellectual and ran his campaign accordingly. His speeches were challenging and intelligent. They attracted praise and attention around the world. Unfortunately, they did not attract U.S. voters. Americans did not want to work so hard to relate to their president. Voters rejected Stevenson's candidacy in favor of Ike in 1952 and again in 1956.

Despite losing his bid for the presidency, Stevenson made many contributions to U.S. politics and history. He wrote several books, including *Major Campaign Speeches* (1952), *Call to Greatness* (1954), and *Looking Outward: Years of Crisis at the United Nations* (1963).

A Young Girl's Diary

World War II was more than a battle between soldiers. Ordinary people had to find ways to survive the fighting and the **Holocaust**. A young Jewish girl named Anne Frank was in Germany in 1929, but she and her family moved to Amsterdam, in the Netherlands. They were living there when Germany invaded the country and began to persecute its Jewish citizens. Afraid of being captured or killed, the Franks, along with four others, went into hiding in a secret room behind a bookcase in 1942. They lived this way until 1944, when their hiding place was discovered. All of them were taken to concentration camps. Anne died in a concentration camp in Belsen, Germany, less than a year later. All that remained of Anne was her diary, which had been safely hidden.

"In spite of everything, I still believe people are really good at heart."

from Anne Frank's diary

■ As a young girl, Anne Frank wrote one of the most important books of all time.

It described with humor and optimism her two years in hiding. The book was published in 1947 in Europe and then appeared in the U.S. in English in 1952. *Anne Frank: The Diary of a Young Girl* gave Americans a look at the horrors of the war and the strength of a child to find the best in her situation. The book became required reading in many schools.

UP CLOSE AND PERSONAL

■ One of the most popular magazines on fifties newsstands was *Photoplay*. It lured 1.2 million readers to its pages each issue. This and other fan magazines featured the lives and loves of movie stars. Much of the content was born from publicity stunts between the magazines and movie studios. A leading man or woman seen in such positive light in the publications could only boost ratings and the amount of money made at theaters. Still, this did not stop millions of Americans from spending twenty cents to find out about the month's romances, heartbreaks, and successes of their favorite stars. As the end of the decade neared, movie studios began to fall to the power of television. As they fell, so did the magazines that supported them. The magazines soon switched from printing favorable stories to running scandalous ones.

Catcher in the Rye

J.D. Salinger wrote stories in the popular *New Yorker* magazine for years. He gained hero status with his first novel, *Catcher in the Rye* (1951). The story of a disillusioned teenager captured the imagination of readers around the world. People could relate to the young man named Holden Caulfield, who did not know what he wanted to do and was frustrated by the "phonies" he met every day. Salinger created a realistic character in this alienated young man. He was viewed as an honorary teenager for capturing how millions of young people were feeling. Some people criticized the book for its use of swear words and its candid look at adult issues. That made it even more of a favorite among rebel teenagers. The book brought Salinger more attention than he expected or wanted. He was a very private person, and the success of *Catcher in the Rye* pushed him to leave Manhattan for a quieter life in New Hampshire. He wrote a few more books during the 1960s and then essentially disappeared from the public eye. He refused interviews and even sued to have a biography about him stopped. In 2000, Salinger's daughter published a book about her life and what it was like growing up with J.D. Salinger as a father.

WORLD FOCUS

TOLKIEN IS LORD OF THE RINGS
British professor J.R.R. Tolkien introduced the world to a society of dragons, monsters, wizards, and hobbits. In 1937, The Hobbit *was published. It was immediately successful and has appeared on children's recommended reading lists ever since. The publisher liked Tolkien's story so much that he asked if the writer could create a sequel to it. Tolkien set out to write a fantasy story that grew into three separate books. In 1954,* The Fellowship of the Ring *was the first in Tolkien's "The Lord of the Rings" trilogy, which also included* The Two Towers *and* The Return of the King. *Through the years, the "Lord of the Rings" books have become favorites of readers all over the world.*

Mickey Spillane

In the 1950s, book publishers were afraid that television would destroy their industry. They were amazed to find that book sales increased by 53 percent through the decade. People stayed home to watch television programs, but once their shows were over, it was too late to go out and too early to go to bed. People read instead. To meet the new demand for books, publishers began producing inexpensive paperbacks. Some of these books sold for only a quarter. About 350 million books had been sold in 1958. Riding the wave of popularity was detective-fiction writer Mickey Spillane. After writing several stories for magazines, Spillane penned his first novel, *I, the Jury,* in just nine days. The hero of the book, Mike Hammer, was a tough ladies' man whom American readers adored. Hammer was strong not only with his fists and guns but also with his sense of justice. Readers bought about 27 million copies of Spillane's novels, including *My Gun is Quick* (1950), *One Lonely Night* (1951), and *Kiss Me Deadly* (1952).

Fictional Science

Science-fiction writer Ray Bradbury was plagued by nightmares and scary fantasies when he was a child. Later, he drew from these experiences to write his stories. Many of his works explored people's destructive habits and how they chose technology over morality. His 1950 novel *The Martian Chronicles* was the story of people who set up a colony on Mars. It brought him instant recognition and became one of his best-known works. *Fahrenheit 451* was another hit book for Bradbury. Published in 1953, this novel described a futuristic society in which books are forbidden. Other popular Bradbury novels include *The Illustrated Man* (1951), *Dandelion Wine* (1957), and *Something Wicked This Way Comes* (1962). In his career, Bradbury wrote more than 500 short stories, plays, novels, and poems.

■ Many of Ray Bradbury's literary works were made into movies.

Nuclear Energy

Six years after atom bombs destroyed Hiroshima and Nagasaki, U.S. scientists found another way to use atomic power. On December 29, 1951, the U.S. Atomic Energy Commission announced that it had found a peaceful use for nuclear energy. Experiments at the Arco, Idaho, nuclear reactor had led to new sources of energy. The heat from the reactor boiled water, and the steam that resulted powered a turbine. Scientists had generated a steady stream of electricity using nuclear power. This success gave them hope that they had discovered an inexpensive energy source—one that would break the country's dependence on fossil fuels such as coal and petroleum. Nuclear power stations were later built in other countries, including France. However, the high costs of building and maintaining these plants prevented nuclear energy from becoming a main power source in many countries.

Medical Hero

Thousands of children contracted poliomyelitis, or polio, each year in the 1940s and early 1950s. This disease attacked muscles and caused paralysis. There was no way to protect people against this contagious disease.

Dr. Jonas Salk began experimenting with ways to prevent polio in 1947. Most vaccines were made from weakened but live strains of whatever disease they were fighting. This was too risky with polio. Salk used dead polio viruses to try to beat the disease. By 1952, the doctor had created a vaccine that stopped polio. He and his staff were injected with the vaccine, and public trials began in 1954. The following year, Salk's vaccine was licensed. It calmed worldwide fears of the disease. Americans watched with relief as the number of polio cases continued to drop.

■ Dr. Jonas Salk's discovery has saved millions of lives around the world.

GENETIC BREAKTHROUGH

■ In 1953, American biochemist James Watson and English biophysicist Francis Crick figured out the structure of deoxyribonucleic acid, or DNA. This substance carries the genetic code—instructions for every living cell. In April, Crick and Watson published their discovery in the British scientific journal *Nature*. Their findings marked the birth of modern genetic science and earned them the Nobel Prize for Medicine in 1962.

PILTDOWN HOAX

The Piltdown Man fossil was unearthed near Piltdown, England, and reported in 1912. This archaeological find thrilled scientists. It also turned the world's understanding of evolution upside down. The skull found seemed to fill the gap between the evolution from apes to man. The finding caused a great deal of controversy and debate around the world. Then, in 1953, the skull was proven to be a hoax. New methods of dating artifacts led scientists to determine that the so-called Piltdown Man was really made from the jaw bone of an orangutan and the skull of a human. The two were put together, stained to look old, and buried to make it appear that they went together. After testing, scientists found that the bones were from two different ages. Some people blamed Charles Dawson for the fraud. He had found the fossils in the first place. Others said Dr. Arthur Smith Woodward was involved. They said the finding supported his theories. In the end, the truth was never uncovered, and Piltdown Man was disregarded.

Power Unleashed

On November 1, 1952, a three-mile-wide cloud developed above the Marshall Islands in the northcentral Pacific Ocean. It was the first test of a hydrogen bomb. The bomb exploded with the power of 10 million tons of dynamite, and it was 500 times more powerful than the bomb dropped on Hiroshima. Physicist Edward Teller, leader of the project, was thrilled with the bomb's success, but not everyone shared his enthusiasm. Atomic scientists J. Robert Oppenheimer, who had directed the development of the first atomic bomb, and Enrico

■ The hydrogen superbomb caused a stir around the world. People were afraid of its power.

Fermi, who first thought of creating such a thermonuclear superbomb, were against the bomb on moral grounds. Oppenheimer was considered a threat and, after McCarthy's trials accused him of being a communist, he lost his security clearance for the project. Despite concerns, President Truman ordered the Atomic Energy Commission to create the hydrogen bomb, or H-bomb, as quickly as possible. Americans tested three more H-bombs in 1954 and another seventeen in 1955.

Queens of the Court

American tennis players made international news in the 1950s. Maureen Connolly won her first National Women's title in 1951 at the age of 16. The following year, she won at Wimbledon and went on to defend her U.S. title. Then, in 1953, she became the first woman and second person ever to win the Grand Slam—top honors at the British, U.S., Australian, and French championships all in one year. Connolly continued to shine in 1954, winning the French and Wimbledon championships. Before the U.S. championships, she had a serious horseback-riding accident that ended her career. She passed on her tennis knowledge and skills through coaching others.

Althea Gibson was another star athlete in the fifties. In 1950, she played in the previously all-white tennis circuit in New York. Then in 1957, she became the first African American to win the prestigious Wimbledon tournament. Gibson also claimed titles at the French, Italian, U.S., and Australian Opens. She was named the Female Athlete of the Year in 1957. The following year, Gibson repeated her reign as the Wimbledon and U.S. national champion. Tennis was not her only strength—she joined the Ladies Professional Golf Association in 1963.

> "This is the player of the year. He might be the player of all the years since baseball has been played."
>
> *New York Post* columnist Jimmy Cannon

Willie Mays

On May 25, 1951, the New York Giants turned their eyes to rookie Willie Mays to help them win games. The team expected great things from this young, talented ballplayer, and so did the fans. When Mays got up to bat for the first time, he struck out. In the next twenty-six trips to home plate, he got only one hit. Fans turned their backs on him, but Mays soon caught their attention. He suddenly began to live up to everyone's expectations. He caught, threw, and batted with dazzling talent and was named Rookie of the Year in 1951. For the next two seasons, Mays served in the U.S.

■ Willie Mays was inducted into the Hall of Fame in 1979.

Army and then came back better than ever. He continued to amaze fans as he led the Giants to a World Series victory in 1954. That year, he was honored with the title Player of the Year. He led the league in stolen bases from 1956 through 1959 and led the National League in home runs in 1955, 1962, 1964, and 1965. When he retired in 1973, Mays had been the first player to hit 300 home runs and steal 300 bases. He was also the first National League player to hit 600 home runs in his career. He is considered one of the best baseball players ever.

Young Girl Takes on the World

Figure skater Tenley Albright knew all about hard work and determination. Her road to the top of the skating world was not an easy one. She overcame polio and fought her way to the top. For six years, she used skating exercises to battle the crippling disease. Then, in 1952, Albright took home a silver medal at the Olympic Games. She knew she could do better, and she proved it in February 1953. This 17-year-old from Boston became the first American to win the world figure skating championship.

In 1956, Albright had another chance to prove that she was the best in the world. She did not disappoint. Despite an ankle injury, Albright became the first American woman to win an Olympic gold medal in figure skating.

■ Terry Sawchuk guards his net against both puck and player.

Detroit on Top

Canadian teams had dominated hockey through the 1940s. In the 1950s, the Detroit Red Wings changed that. Despite an injured Gordie Howe, the Red Wings started out the decade with a Stanley Cup win in 1950. Howe recovered through the off-season and returned to the team, but they could not defend their championship. In 1952, Terry Sawchuk made his goaltending debut in the finals and was a star. He shut out the Montreal Canadiens in two games and held them to only two goals in total during the four-game series. The Red Wings had won another Stanley Cup. After losing the title to Montreal in 1953, the Red Wings came back to win it again in 1954. This time, the team successfully defended its title with another Stanley Cup win in 1955. Then the streak ended for decades. The Red Wings would not win another Stanley Cup until 1997.

GOLF LEGEND

■ Golfer Ben Hogan had been the leading money winner several seasons during the 1940s. He was thought to be one of the greatest golfers ever. In 1949, Hogan was nearly killed when his car was hit by a bus. Doctors thought he might not walk well again. He surprised everyone. Only seventeen months later, in 1950, Hogan won his second U.S. Open championship. He won the tournament again in 1951. Then, in 1953, he crushed the record for the tournament by five strokes. That year, he went on to win the British Open as well. Throughout his career, Hogan won more than sixty tournaments and set a standard for future golfers.

Yankee Pride

The New York Yankees won eight division pennants and six World Series championships between 1950 and 1959. They did so with the leadership of two All-Star players—Yogi Berra and Mickey Mantle. Berra was a famed Yankees catcher. He played in fifteen All-Star games in a row and was the league's Most Valuable Player in 1951, 1954, and 1955. Berra held several records, including the career home-run record for catchers. He won fourteen pennants and ten World Series championships in his incredible eighteen-year career—more than any other player. He was famous for his sayings, which he spouted off behind the plate to distract batters, entertain umpires, and inspire his teammates. His determination and never-say-die attitude was summed up by his famous adage, "It ain't over 'til it's over." He retired in 1965 but stayed a part of the game as a coach and manager.

Mickey Mantle had big shoes to fill when he replaced Joe DiMaggio in centerfield in 1951. Despite injuries and a bone inflammation in his leg, Mantle led the league six times in runs scored and four times in home runs. Mantle held the batting title in 1956 and won the **Triple Crown** the same year. He was voted Most Valuable Player in 1956, 1957, and 1962. Through the twelve World Series championships in which he competed, Mantle set records for most runs, most home runs, most runs batted in, and total bases batted in regular season and play-off competition. Mantle retired in 1969. Both he and Berra became baseball legends and were inducted into the Baseball Hall of Fame.

■ **Mickey Mantle hit eighteen World Series home runs— a record.**

Perfect Pitching

Pitcher Don Larsen had struggled to become a starting pitcher with the New York Yankees after being sent back to the minor leagues in 1955. Manager Casey Stengel believed in Larsen and knew he would come through for the team. After a few disappointing games in the 1956 World Series, fans demanded that Larsen sit on the bench. Stengel had other ideas.

Larsen started the fifth game of the series against Brooklyn on October 8. As the innings passed, people realized that no one had hit safely off Larsen yet. He had not walked a batter, either. Could he become the first ever to pitch a perfect game in the World Series? Many thought it impossible but held their breath anyway as Larsen kept throwing strikes. As he delivered a final strike to end the game, catcher Yogi Berra ran to the mound to celebrate. Larsen had done it! The Yankees were the champions, and Larsen had made history. He set a record by pitching the first no-hitter in World Series history. He also pitched a perfect game— not one batter had reached first base. Throughout nine whole innings of play, Larsen threw only ninety-seven pitches.

Marciano a Knock-out

Rocco "Rocky" Marciano began boxing in the U.S. Army and then launched a professional boxing career in 1947. In 1951, the strongman cried after knocking out Joe Louis, his boyhood hero. In September 1952, Marciano became the world heavyweight champion by knocking out Jersey Joe Walcott. Marciano had been losing that fight, but he came back with a flurry of punches that showed both his strength and his incredible determination. Between 1953 and 1955, Marciano defended his title successfully six times. He retired in 1956 when he was 33 years old. During his professional career, he won forty-three professional bouts by knockout. His final tally was forty-nine wins, no losses. Marciano was the only heavyweight champion to have a perfect record.

■ Rocky Marciano's right hook was a powerful weapon.

BASKETBALL DYNASTY

■ The National Basketball Association (NBA) was formed in 1950, and the Minneapolis Lakers were part of it. That season, the team battled the Rochester Royals for the division title and breezed through the semifinals. With players such as George Mikan, Jim Pollard, Bud Grant, and Vern Mikkelsen, the Lakers seemed unstoppable. They beat the Syracuse Nationals to win the first NBA championship and their second championship in a row. Most critics pegged the Lakers as the favorites the following year, but the Royals clinched the division title. The Lakers were not discouraged. They came back in 1952 and 1953 to beat the New York Knickerbockers for top honors. The Lakers were the first repeat champions in the league. The Lakers were a team to fear in the NBA. In 1954, they defended their championship again with a win against Syracuse.

At the end of the season, the league introduced the 24-second time limit to shoot and a foul limit per player and per team. These new elements of the game, along with the loss of veteran players, hurt the Lakers. Their dynasty was over. They did not win another championship in the 1950s.

NEW WAY TO SHOP

■ The Northland Center near Detroit, Michigan, became a haven for shoppers in 1954. It was the first in a new type of shopping experience. Die-hard shoppers no longer needed to travel outside from store to store. This new shopping mall featured hundreds of stores under one roof on several different levels of a building. There were restaurants, child-care facilities, arcades, and free parking. The Northland Center was designed by architect Victor Gruen. The shopping center attracted thousands of people immediately. City officials hoped that similar malls would breathe life into some run-down cities, or areas of cities, throughout the country.

Act of Heroism

In 1954, the U.S. Supreme Court ruled that keeping people separate because of race was unconstitutional. It took officials in many states several years before they began to **integrate** society. The ruling did not hold much weight. In the south, much of society, including schools and buses, was still separated according to race. On December 1, 1955, an African-American seamstress named Rosa Parks refused to give up her seat to a white man when traveling home in an Alabama bus. She was sitting in the middle section of the bus, where African Americans could sit if their seats were not needed by whites. Rosa was arrested for refusing to give up her seat when a white passenger demanded it. This led African Americans to protest. They supported a bus **boycott** led by Baptist minister and civil rights activist Martin Luther King, Jr. The boycott lasted for 382 days, costing the bus company a great deal of money. In 1956, the issue of segregated seating on buses was brought before a federal court. The court ruled that such a policy was unconstitutional. King and many others continued their fight against discrimination into the 1960s. Their efforts led to the Civil Rights Acts of 1964 and 1968.

Segregated Schools

African Americans tested the Supreme Court ruling and tried to integrate U.S. schools. In April 1956, the courts ruled that Autherine Lucy, an African-American student, should be able to enroll at the University of Alabama. White students rioted, and Lucy was suspended for her own protection. The National Association for the Advancement of Colored People (NAACP) brought the case to court. The university refused to allow Lucy back, despite a federal court order to reinstate her.

Arkansas, like Alabama, did not support integration. Despite a federal order on September 3, 1957, Arkansas's state governor

sent police to stop African-American students from entering Little Rock High School. Three weeks later, President Eisenhower sent troops to enforce school desegregation in the state. Nine African-American children, with federal troops on either side of them,

■ U.S. troops escort an African-American student to school.

entered their new school to learn alongside white children. This was the beginning of desegregation, but it was well into the 1960s and 1970s before integration was accepted in the South.

Rebel Youth

In the mid-1950s, big city slums gave rise to a notorious young figure—the rebel. The number of crimes committed by teenagers soared. In 1956 in New York, the number of teen murderers jumped 26 percent from the previous year. A 36 percent increase in car thefts and 92 percent rise in weapon possession charges were attributed to young rebels. But police figured that only one in ten gangs in New York, Chicago, and Los Angeles was violent. The rest were rebelling against authority through their clothing, language, and habits rather than through serious criminal actions.

Gangs spread to smaller cities and rural areas as well. Hollywood picked up on the trend and released rebel movies, including *Teenage Doll*, *High School Confidential*, and Marlon Brando's *Wild One*. Soon, teen boys and girls were wearing black leather jackets, tight jeans,

and tattoos. Some even carried switchblades. They would rumble, or fight, with other gangs in their areas for anything from turf to girls. The teens abandoned their given names in favor of nicknames such as Snake, Diablo (which is "devil" in Spanish), Bebop, and Hatchet. They fell under gangs with similar names, including the Vikings, the Cobras, the Centurions, and the Crusaders. Many young Americans battled for control of the streets throughout the decade.

SUBURBIA

Millions of Americans made the trek from the city to the suburbs in the 1950s. Nearly 1.4 million new homes were built in 1950 alone. People wanted larger homes to accommodate their growing families—the U.S. was experiencing an incredible baby boom after the war. These suburbs were often referred to as Babyville, because of the number of children who lived there. Many Americans also hoped that this move would bring them higher social status and the "right" kind of friends. They hosted and attended cocktail parties, enrolled their children in dance and music lessons, Girl Scouts or Cub Scouts, and signed them up for Little League. Still, life in the suburbs also had disadvantages. People had to brave rickety railroads or bumper-to-bumper traffic on highways to get to work every day. Taxes were higher in order to support the schools that were needed, and parents had to hire babysitters for seventy-five cents an hour because their relatives often lived too far away. Americans flocked to the outskirts for the backyard barbecues and the sense of community.

Consumer Revolution

In the 1950s, it seemed that everyone had something to sell. Selling became an art form mastered by door-to-door salespeople. Designers studied the most attractive colors for products, what size they should be, and how much people would consider paying for them. Some of the most successful door-to-door salespeople sold vacuums, other cleaning equipment, encyclopedias, and make-up. The Avon lady and the Fuller Brush man became icons of the fifties.

To influence millions of people at once, companies began using the new medium—television. Advertisements on television boosted sales quickly and drastically. Having the product endorsed by a celebrity or expert helped even more. Soon, the products being designed were linked closely with marketing. Everything had to have selling points to set it apart from the competition. In self-service supermarkets, consumers walked the aisles and stopped at eye-catching displays. Companies worked to catch consumers' attention so that their products would sell.

Fall and Rise of Eisenhower's Economy

President Eisenhower was a firm believer that local, not federal, governments should have control over their own affairs. He reduced taxes and called for cuts in federal spending in an attempt to balance the budget. He also removed wage and price controls to let the economy flourish on its own. At the same time, he expanded Social Security benefits and created a new department to handle health, education, and welfare. In the fifties, Americans were hit with rising living costs, budget **deficits**, and lower agricultural prices. In 1953, a nearly two-year economic recession swept the country. The slump was ended by the Revenue Act of 1954. This cut taxes and relaxed credit. President Eisenhower also increased federal spending on roadways and schools. The economy rebounded and slowly began to grow again.

In the late 1950s, Americans experienced some hard times. Stock prices began to **fluctuate** in 1957, beginning a 9-month economic slump. This came after several years of unheard-of prosperity across the nation. At the beginning of 1958, a recession swept the country. By the middle of the year, the economy had grown even worse. Unemployment rates skyrocketed. More than 5 million Americans were without jobs in June. This was the highest level of unemployment since World War II. By the end of the year, the downturn had been stabilized, and the economy set out on a slow road to recovery.

Friedman's Philosophy

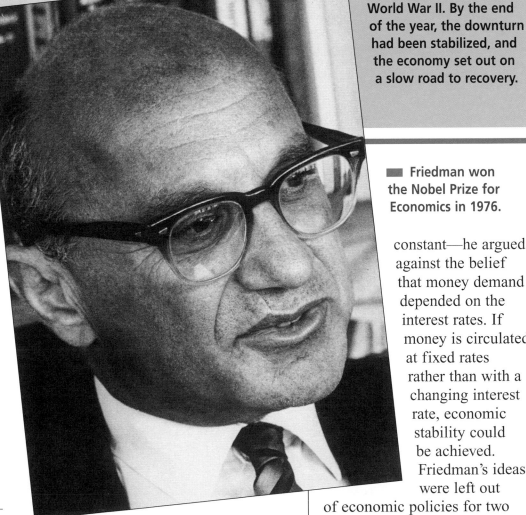

Friedman won the Nobel Prize for Economics in 1976.

Economist Milton Friedman fought the U.S. government's economic position. In 1957, his book *A Theory of the Consumption Function*, criticized Western economic policies after World War II. Friedman and his associates—called the "Chicago School" for their connection to the University of Chicago—wanted to put **monetarism** back into practice. They argued that money supply and interest rates were the keys to economic growth, not government spending and taxation. Friedman's theory held that the demand for money and the speed at which it circulated in society were constant—he argued against the belief that money demand depended on the interest rates. If money is circulated at fixed rates rather than with a changing interest rate, economic stability could be achieved. Friedman's ideas were left out of economic policies for two decades. By the 1980s, presidents and prime ministers around the world were looking at his theories when trying to improve their country's economies.

■ Arms are raised at the historic merger between the AFL and the CIO.

Union Power

A huge union superpower took shape in December 1955. The deal was pushed through by George Meany, a strong union man from the pre-Depression days. The American Federation of Labor (AFL) united with the Congress of Industrial Organizations (CIO). Together these organizations represented about 16 million U.S. union members. The merger had been in the works since 1952. Dwight Eisenhower had become the first Republican president in twenty years. Labor unions had traditionally backed Democratic candidates, whom they trusted

to look after their needs. This change in leadership heightened the labor unions' feeling that a united front was needed in dealing with the government. George Meany was elected president of the AFL-CIO and served in that position for twenty-five years. During his run, he expelled the Teamsters Union from the organization. The Teamsters was the most powerful and largest union since the war, and it was kicked out of the AFL-CIO for corruption in 1957. It took thirty years for the union to shake off its shady reputation and disreputable leaders and be allowed back into the AFL-CIO.

Nerves of Steel

After World War II, the U.S. experienced a period of severe economic **inflation**. This caused workers to go on strike in many major industries. President Truman knew that of all the industries, he could not afford to allow a steel strike. The war effort in Korea depended on steel production. Steelworkers had been working without a contract since the beginning of the year, and a strike date had been set for April 9, 1952. Hours before the strike was to begin, Truman took action. He ordered Secretary of Commerce Charles Sawyer to take control of the steel mills in order to ensure that war production continued. This was only a temporary solution. The Supreme Court ruled against the president's seizure, saying it was unconstitutional. After the verdict, the planned steel strike was carried out. Steelworkers left the factories and stayed off the job for fifty-three days until an agreement was reached. Another steel strike hit in 1959. The Supreme Court ordered workers back to work and President Eisenhower reminded both sides of their obligation to resolve the issues. The strike had lasted 116 days— the longest steel strike to date.

Dressing Up Dresses

Women looked to accessories to dress up their wardrobes. Some young women pasted rhinestones and stick-on pins and brooches on their skin for a different look. This way, even in strapless dresses, their shoulders could glitter and sparkle. For some women, **versatility** was the answer. Pop-it necklaces were a great way to get many necklaces in one. Women could lengthen or shorten the beaded string by popping it apart and adding or taking out beads. These necklaces could go from waist-long to chokers in a matter of seconds. Other extras, including pearl necklaces, were made popular by television's June Cleaver. Hats, which had been an essential part of a woman's wardrobe in previous years, became less important in the 1950s. However, many women still wore hats and gloves to church or the synagogue. Younger women often decided to go hatless.

Davy Crockett Style

On December 15, 1954, Walt Disney's weekly television show *Disneyland* created hysteria with young people. Children could not get enough of Davy Crockett. Fess Parker starred as the lovable Davy Crockett—and kicked off a $100 million market for his coonskin hats. Many children between 5 and 15 years old had to have an authentic coonskin cap. Stores could not keep enough Davy Crockett lunch boxes, caps, T-shirts, bathing suits, and even guitars on the shelves. An album called *The Ballad of Davy Crockett* sold 4 million copies. Davy Crockett was everywhere, but only for a while. By the summer of 1955, the Davy Crockett phase had fizzled, leaving stores with boxes of unsold items.

■ Davy Crockett was truly "King of the Wild Frontier."

GUYS LIVEN UP

■ For the first time, pink became popular. It had always appeared on women's undergarments or dresses, but it had never been introduced into men's wardrobes. In the fifties, the traditional men's charcoal gray suits gave way to color. Pink ties and hatbands began to creep into closets across the country. Freed from their fashion prisons, men took advantage of the new styles. They wore Bermuda shorts and sported thin Colonel ties to shake up suits. High school students went back to school in pleated rogue pants. These pants had a white stripe along the side and were often worn with a matching white belt. Boys and men also bought closets full of baggy pegged pants to wear to dance hall sock hops.

Style Guide

Teen styles were fun in the 1950s. Blue jeans were a must in every American's wardrobe. They were the ultimate piece of casual clothing. During World War II, jeans had been sold only to people employed in defense work. By the fifties, everyone wore them. They became U.S. fashion symbols throughout the world. Jeans were often rolled up so that there were thick cuffs at mid-calf length. Another casual style was short shorts, which often had rolled cuffs as well. This daring style showed much of a woman's leg.

For dressier occasions, poodle skirts were the first choice for many young U.S. women. Crinolines

■ Fifties style for her meant fun colors and flare skirts.

caused these skirts to flare out, showing off the poodle sewn toward the bottom of the skirt. The short socks and running shoes that often accompanied poodle skirts made the outfit comfortable and easy to move around in. Hair tied back in a ponytail with a ribbon finished off the teen look. Some older women preferred straighter styles. Tight-fitting skirts with tailor-fitted jackets were an important part of a woman's wardrobe. Short gloves were often worn to accent the classy outfits.

Head-to-Toe Fashion

Both men and women brought new hairstyles to the fifties fashion scene. Many men often went with the ducktail style. This haircut required that one side be folded into the other, much like a duck's tail. Hollywood stars made this hairdo a must. The style was a fad, but not everyone liked it. In February 1957, a Massachusetts school stopped allowing its students to wear their hair in a ducktail. Crewcuts or flattops, on the other hand, were steady favorites with young and old. The military-inspired style was short and squared off at the sides. Parents approved of this clean-cut fashion.

Women also introduced new hairstyles in the fifties. The poodle was worn by both young and mature women. This short hairstyle was permed into tight curls—much like a poodle's curly locks. Hollywood stars such as Peggy Ann Garner, Ann Sothern, and Faye Emerson, helped make this look popular. Other women preferred longer, straighter styles. It took great efforts to make the ends of their hair curl upwards.

With their heads looking great, Americans looked for new styles for the feet. Late in the decade, stiletto heels became popular. These shoes had pointed heels and narrow toes. Despite protests from doctors, who said these shoes could harm feet, and from flooring specialists, who blamed stilettos for dents and holes in carpets and wood floors, many Americans insisted on having at least one pair of these shoes. Sensible saddle shoes and penny loafers remained popular throughout the decade.

Braceros Come to America

Braceros, including children, worked long hours in U.S. fields.

During World War II, the agricultural industry had suffered from a shortage of workers. To help supply workers, the government came to an agreement to allow temporary employees from Mexico, Canada, Jamaica, Barbados, and the Bahamas to work in the fields. These workers were called braceros. The agreement carried past the war and was still in place in the 1950s. The Commission on Migratory Labor in Agriculture examined the situation. It criticized the U.S. government for not protecting the living and working standards of these temporary immigrants. Rather than recruiting in Mexico, many illegal immigrants already living in the country were given braceros status. This, the Commission said, went against immigration policies and the spirit of the agreement.

In 1951, Public Law 78 was introduced. It limited braceros to Mexico. The following year, the Immigration and Nationality Act included a provision for limited use of other temporary workers, mostly West Indians. This did not represent large numbers and was never more than 30,000 workers. The Act also specified that U.S. workers had to be sought first and that braceros had to be paid the standard wage. The use of braceros increased through the 1950s until it waned and was stopped in 1964. There was a great deal of debate over whether braceros were given all that the agreements promised, such as fair wages, safety on the job, and good treatment. One thing came out of using braceros— the number of illegal **aliens** in the U.S. declined greatly.

IMMIGRATION QUOTAS

The U.S. Senate passed the Immigration and Nationality Act in June 1952. This was done despite President Truman's veto of the legislation. He felt that the Act would "intensify the repressive and inhumane aspects of our immigration procedures." The Immigration and Nationality Act restructured the system and restricted the number of people coming into the country. It set maximum numbers of people who could enter the U.S. from certain areas of the world. Total immigration was set at 154,657 people per year. Visas to enter the country were now given first to those immigrants with a high level of education, technical training, or specialized experience that would be useful to American society.

Illegal Immigration

Despite the braceros program of the 1950s, many Mexicans entered the U.S. illegally. They could not meet the requirements to apply for citizenship or were not able to work as braceros. There was a great deal of discussion about how to handle the problem. Many Americans were angry that these people could come into their country and take jobs meant for legal immigrants or U.S. citizens. Others feared that these illegal aliens might bring new diseases with them because they did not go through the proper immigration channels. Stopping illegal immigration meant plugging the holes in the Mexican-American border. This would prove very difficult to do. Instead, the government made a motion to make it illegal for employers to hire illegal aliens. Congress did not pass it.

For the next few years, many organizations tried to find a way to stop illegal immigration. In 1954, the Immigration and Naturalization Service (INS) set a military-style operation

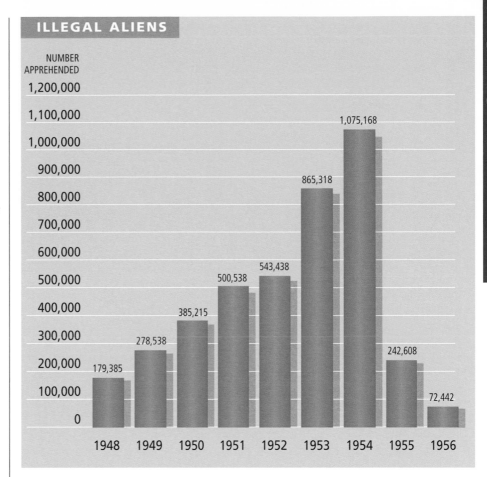

ILLEGAL ALIENS

NUMBER APPREHENDED

- 1948: 179,385
- 1949: 278,538
- 1950: 385,215
- 1951: 500,538
- 1952: 543,438
- 1953: 865,318
- 1954: 1,075,168
- 1955: 242,608
- 1956: 72,442

in motion. It began in California and swept across the Southwest. INS agents picked up thousands of illegal aliens by using roadblocks and by raiding growers known to hire aliens. Agents also hit Midwestern cities, including Chicago. Those without the proper documents

■ The number of illegal aliens apprehended in the U.S. declined greatly between 1954 and 1955.

were **deported**. Meanwhile, the Border Patrol did what it could to plug the holes at the border. Countless illegal immigrants remained undetected in the U.S.

Immigration in the Fifties

Many people around the world wanted to make the U.S. their home. In the years between 1951 and 1960, more than 2.3 million people moved to the U.S. from other countries. This chart shows where some of these immigrants came from and their estimated numbers.

Country	Number	Country	Number
Germany	477,800	Ireland	48,400
Canada	378,000	Central America	44,800
Mexico	299,800	Hungary	36,600
Great Britain	202,800	Norway	22,900
Italy	185,500	Sweden	21,700
Caribbean	123,100	Philippines	19,300
South America	91,600	Africa	14,100
Cuba	78,900	Oceania	13,000
Austria	67,100	China	9,700

Dick Clark

In 1952, Dick Clark was spinning records for a Philadelphia radio station. Within four years, the young disc jockey was promoted to a television show called *Bandstand*, which later became known as *American Bandstand*. The show was a hit. Clark brought the hottest rock-and-roll stars to the show, and they performed while a studio full of teenagers danced along. The regular teen dancers became household names across the country as well. Some even had their own fan clubs.

Clark's weekly top songs influenced which records teenagers bought. An appearance on *American Bandstand* could launch a singer into stardom and

boost record sales by hundreds of thousands. Clark asked the dancers their opinions about new songs and rated them. The best songs had a great beat and were easy to dance to. *American Bandstand* became the longest-running television program in U.S. history. It aired for more than four decades, featuring such stars as Bill Haley and His Comets, Buddy Holly, the Mamas and the Papas, James Brown, the Jackson Five, the Village People, Blondie, Billy Joel, and Madonna.

■ Dick Clark's popularity helped make *American Bandstand* legendary.

BROTHERLY SUCCESS

■ Two Kentucky siblings, Don and Phil, influenced how future musicians sounded. The Everly Brothers' harmonies, acoustic guitar melodies, and rock and roll beat were unparalleled. The brothers had been singing together on their parents' radio show since they were 6 and 8 years old. In 1957, they made it big. Their first single, "Bye Bye Love," was a smash hit, and the album sold more than 1 million copies. The brothers were instant stars. They appeared on such career-makers as *The Ed Sullivan Show* and *American Bandstand*. For their contribution to music, The Everly Brothers were inducted into the Rock and Roll Hall of Fame in 1986.

Rock and Roll Invasion

In the mid-1950s, rock and roll invaded the U.S. This new style of music was a combination of folk, blues, and country—and it was played fast. A Cleveland disc jockey called Alan Freed promoted this new music and named it. The rhythm made listeners want to sway, or rock, with the beat, so he called it "rock and roll." Bill Haley and His Comets were among rock's pioneers. Their 1955 hit "Rock Around the Clock" was the first rock-and-roll song to achieve wide success. Chuck Berry was another pioneer. His hits "Maybellene,"

"Johnny B. Goode," and "Roll Over, Beethoven" made him a star. Today, musicians continue to try to imitate Berry's musical style.

Other artists, including Fats Domino, Buddy Holly, Jerry Lee Lewis, and Little Richard, helped shape U.S. rock and roll. They often wrote their own songs about issues that mattered to teenagers. As the sixties replaced the fifties, rock changed. The new rockers used session musicians and sang songs written by hired writers. Still, rock and roll in the U.S. kept its distinctly American feel.

The King of Rock and Roll

In 1956, Elvis Presley entered the rock-and-roll scene with a sound that was a combination of traditional blues, gospel, and country and western music. His albums sold millions of copies, and his appearance on *The Ed Sullivan Show* attracted 54 million viewers. Young fans screamed and fainted over him, but adults were not impressed. They thought that his hip-swinging dance moves were vulgar and that his effect on young women was evil. They did not care that Presley said his prayers, was polite, and loved his parents. They thought his act was "unfit for a family audience." Teenagers bought about 70 percent of the records in the fifties. They spent their money on Elvis, both at the record stores and at the movie theaters. He starred in many movies in the fifties, including *Blue Hawaii* and *Viva Las Vegas.* By 1960, Presley had sold more than $120 million worth of albums.

■ Elvis Presley was a silver-screen legend as well as "King of Rock and Roll."

FIFTIES SIRENS

■ The fifties brought fame to many talented female singers. The big band era was over and the "girl singers" who were part of large groups branched out on their own. Rosemary Clooney had been singing on the radio since 1945, and she signed a record contract in 1949. In 1951, she was persuaded to record a novelty song called "Come On-a My House." It was an instant success. This started an incredible singing career that lasted through the century.

Brenda Lee was another popular singer. She performed on radio specials and then was invited to sing at a concert given by country star Red Foley. He was amazed at her talent and asked her to sing on his television special. From there, Lee became a superstar. Her first singles, "Jambalaya" and "Dynamite" in 1956, led to several others in later decades.

The Day the Music Died

Buddy Holly, the Big Bopper, and Richie Valens died in Iowa while on their way to a concert in Fargo, North Dakota. Their plane crashed on February 3, 1959. Fans across the country were devastated by the accident. Richie Valens was rock's first Mexican-American hero. Hits including "Donna" and "La Bamba" had launched him into superstardom. The Big Bopper was a disc jockey and songwriter. Most of his songs, including "Chantilly Lace," were novelty tunes. The most famous and well-loved victim of the crash was Buddy Holly. He was a talented pioneer of rock and roll, and he changed the genre. He used rhythm-and-blues beats in the background of his songs, and he was the first to overdub, which allowed him to accompany himself. Holly's songs, "Peggy Sue," "That'll Be the Day," and others soared to the top of the charts and made him a hero. His style influenced many other rock and roll stars.

■ Buddy Holly's style is still mimicked by performers today.

Supporting Coups

In 1951, Iran decided to nationalize the British-owned Anglo-Iranian Oil Company. London asked the U.S. to help. Negotiations failed, and the British looked to the U.S. to support a boycott of Iranian oil. President Truman was not sure if he should support the Iranians or his ally's interests. His **successor**, Dwight Eisenhower, did not face the same problem. He feared Iran would become communist, so he stepped in. The boycott crippled Iran's economy and its nationalist party. To maintain control, Muhammad Mussadegh, Iran's premier, became a dictator. He now counted on the support of the communist Tudeh Party, which was becoming more and more powerful.

In 1953, when Mussadegh insisted that the **Shah** be ousted, even the Tudeh turned against him. The time was perfect for President Eisenhower and British Prime Minister Churchill to act. The Shah had ordered Mussadegh to resign, but he refused to go. His followers rebelled, and the Shah fled. The Central Intelligence Agency (CIA) took charge of the coup. It hired mobs and orchestrated a military revolt. In the course of a week of street fighting, 300 Iranians died, Mussadegh was arrested, and the Shah returned.

■ Many Iranians were angry that the U.S. stopped buying oil from Iran.

Immediately, Iran was ruled by the military. The Anglo-Iranian Oil Company became an international group, and the U.S. held a major stake in the organization. Throughout Iran, anti-American feelings spread and grew stronger.

KHRUSHCHEV STARTS THAW

■ Soviet leader Nikita Khrushchev made a speech in February 1956 about the crimes of Stalin, the dictator who had died in 1953. Until then, no public criticism of the leader had been permitted. Khrushchev spoke of Stalin as a mass murderer and a power-hungry leader who ruled by terror and betrayed communism and the USSR. Krushchev's "secret speech" addressed Stalin's deportation of many national minorities back to their homelands. Khrushchev condemned Stalin for his illegal deeds and the effects his actions had on Soviets. Khrushchev's speech marked the begining of his de-Stalinization efforts. He wanted to improve the standard of living and give citizens more freedom. The secret police became less important to government operations. The USSR, however, remained a communist country. Many people in the West hoped that Khrushchev's new vision would help open relations between the U.S. and the USSR.

Meetings in Geneva

In 1955, the world was settling into post-war life. In May, the USSR agreed to the Austrian State Treaty. This gave Austria its independence, and Soviet troops withdrew from the area. This occupation had been a sore point between the East and West. In July, leaders from Britain, France, and the U.S. met with the Soviet leader in Geneva, Switzerland, to talk about how Austria and the USSR could live together peacefully. President Eisenhower announced that he did not intend to participate in an aggressive war. This relieved citizens of the world. Many feared a nuclear war. The conference also discussed the feeling of hopefulness in the USSR after Stalin's death. In the end, no substantial agreements were reached at these meetings.

The Kitchen Debate

In 1959, Vice President Richard Nixon and Soviet Premier Nikita Khrushchev exchanged heated words in what was to be called the "Kitchen Debate." Nixon flew to Moscow in July to open the American National Exhibition. This was an unusual Soviet presentation of U.S. culture. The visit came just after the U.S. Congress had passed the Captive Nations Resolution, which criticized the Soviet government for the way it treated the countries under its control. Before heading to the exhibition, the two politicians met. The discussion quickly turned into an argument about the U.S. resolution. The men then left to tour the exhibition grounds separately. They met again in the kitchen of a model U.S. home. Khrushchev made fun of the gadgets, including juicers and dishwashers, and said he figured U.S. workers could not afford these luxuries. Nixon struck back, saying that the average American could easily live in this model home. The conversation turned into a debate about communism versus capitalism, right there

■ Despite the firm tone of the Kitchen Debate, both Nixon and Krushchev agreed that each nation could learn from the other.

in the kitchen. Before then, world statesmen had rarely spoken to one another so sharply or so honestly.

Where Did It Happen?

Match the following events with the locations in which they happened:

1. Where Buddy Holly, the Big Bopper, and Richie Valens were headed when they crashed
2. The home of the 1950s Lakers basketball team
3. Nuclear energy experiments held
4. Tenley Albright's hometown
5. Location of Our Lady of Angels school

6. *Dragnet*'s inspiration city
7. The last American state to join the Union
8. Willie May's home field
9. Where Dick Clark started disc jockeying
10. Location of the Northland Center

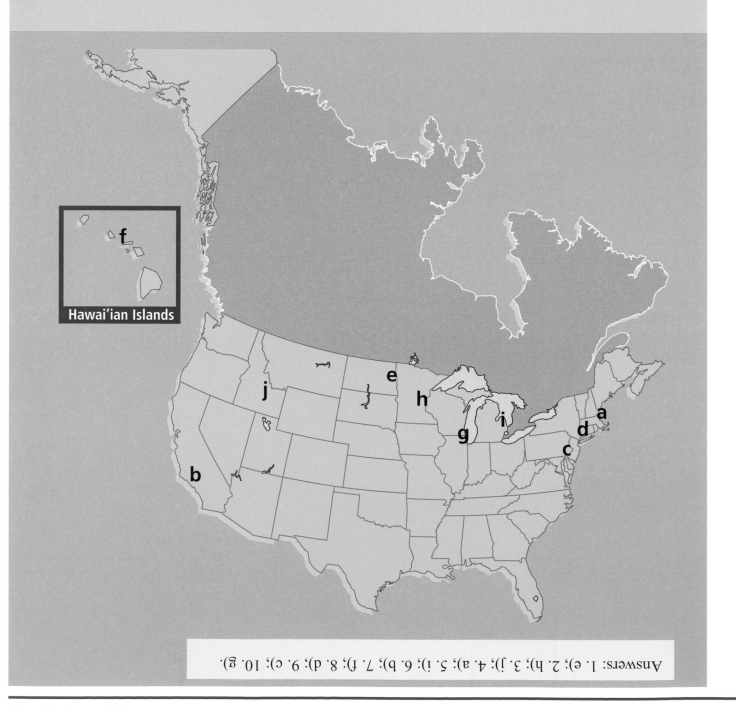

Hawai'ian Islands

True or False

1 Laika was
a) a U.S. space shuttle
b) the first dog in space
c) a style of poetry made popular by beatniks

2 In 1954, President Eisenhower
a) lost the election
b) lost majority control of Congress
c) decided to step down as president

3 The Warsaw Pact
a) gave more land to Poland
b) combined Europe's military
c) brought communist countries together in a treaty

4 Alan Freed was
a) the disc jockey who created the term "rock and roll"
b) a star pitcher for the New York Yankees
c) the first man to climb Mount Everest

5 *Catcher in the Rye*
a) brought more attention than J.D. Salinger wanted
b) was J.D. Salinger's only novel
c) was about senior citizens in Arizona

Answers: 1. b); 2. b); 3. c); 4. a); 5. a).

Newsmakers

Match the newsmakers with their claim to 1950s fame.

1. led H-bomb trials

2. hero in Mickey Spillane books

3. Secretary of Defense

4. first woman to win Grand Slam in tennis

5. pitched a perfect game in the World Series

6. climbed Mount Everest

7. launched anti-communism hearings

8. civil rights activist

9. beatnik writer

10. held organized crime investigation

a) Don Larsen
b) Joseph McCarthy
c) Edmund Hillary
d) Rosa Parks
e) Jack Kerouac
f) Edward Teller
g) Mike Hammer
h) Estes Kafauver
i) Maureen Connolly
j) Charles E. Wilson

Answers: 1. f); 2. g); 3. j); 4. i); 5. a); 6. c); 7. b); 8. d); 9. e); 10. h).

affiliate: associate

aliens: foreigners

apartheid: a policy separating people according to their race, especially in South Africa.

arsonist: a person who intentionally sets fires

boycott: refusing to buy or use

cease-fire: agreement to stop fighting—a truce

censure: strong criticism or blame

collectivization: to move from private to public or collective ownership, for instance, in farming

coup: to seize power illegally or with violence

Creole: descendant of European settlers in the West Indies

deficit: when expenses are more than income

deported: sent back to one's home country

escalated: increased

fluctuate: rise and fall irregularly

fraud: a dishonest trick or deception

guerrilla: a member of a small group fighting independently for a cause

Holocaust: mass murder of Jews by Nazis in World War II

inflation: increase in prices and the fall of money value

integrate: bring together

lofty: noble aims

monetarism: control of the supply of money as a way of stabilizing the economy

provisional: temporary

Shah: king of Iran

successor: a person who comes after another

three-dimensional: showing length, width, and depth

toxic: poisonous

Triple Crown: when a baseball player leads in home runs, runs batted in, and batting average in a season

underworld: professional criminals and their associates

versatility: the ability to be used for many things

Viet Minh: a nationalist independent movement in Vietnam

Here are some book resources and Internet links if you want to learn more about the people, places, and events that made headlines during the 1950s.

Books

Brewster, Todd, and Peter Jennings. *The Century for Young People*. New York: Random House, 1999.

Comden, Betty, *Singin' in the Rain*. London: Lorimer, 1986.

Frank, Anne. *The Diary of a Young Girl*. New York: Bantam Doubleday, 1953.

Internet Links

http://www.laca.org/Maysville/MaysvilleMS/fifties.htm

http://www.magnetplace.com/RETRO

http://www.joesherlock.com/fifties.html

For information about other U.S. subjects, type your key words into a search engine such as Alta Vista or Yahoo!

1950s Index